Birth

A Conscious Choice

By

Hannah M. Bajor, C.N.M., M.S.N., R.N.C.

Certified Bereavement Counselor for Pregnancy Loss

Body-Mind-Spirit-Energetic-Healing Practitioner

Registered General Nurse

Certified Nurse Midwife

3rd Step Ritual Master

Reiki Master

Note for Librarians: a cataloguing record for this book that includes Dewey Decimal Classification and US Library of Congress numbers is available from the Library and Archives of Canada. The complete cataloguing record can be obtained from their online database at:
www.collectionscanada.ca/amicus/index-e.html
ISBN 1-4120-4998-9
Printed in Victoria, BC, Canada

TRAFFORD

Offices in Canada, USA, Ireland, UK and Spain
This book was published on-demand in cooperation with Trafford Publishing. On-demand publishing is a unique process and service of making a book available for retail sale to the public taking advantage of on-demand manufacturing and Internet marketing. On-demand publishing includes promotions, retail sales, manufacturing, order fulfilment, accounting and collecting royalties on behalf of the author.
Book sales for North America and international:
Trafford Publishing, 6E–2333 Government St.,
Victoria, BC v8t 4p4 CANADA
phone 250 383 6864 (toll-free 1 888 232 4444)
fax 250 383 6804; email to orders@trafford.com
Book sales in Europe:
Trafford Publishing (uk) Ltd., Enterprise House, Wistaston Road Business Centre,
Wistaston Road, Crewe, Cheshire cw2 7rp UNITED KINGDOM
phone 01270 251 396 (local rate 0845 230 9601)
facsimile 01270 254 983; orders.uk@trafford.com
Order online at:
www.trafford.com/robots/04-2806.html

10 9 8 7 6

I dedicate this book, to my mother Mrs. Josephine Lynam (Tullamore, County Offaly, Ireland), for being the great woman she is, and for allowing me to enter this planet through her physical vessel. I am forever grateful for all the sacrifices she made and continues to make as a mother and grandmother.

Acknowledgements

I am the empowered person that I am today because of the many people I have met at different stages within my life. I am forever grateful for all of the wonderful support and life lessons brought to me through them.

My favorite quote

There is only one religion,
the religion of Love.
There is only one caste,
the caste of Humanity.
There is only one race,
the Human Race.
Sri Sathya Sai Baba

Table of Contents

CHAPTER 1

▼

Introduction

Ihave been a traditional certified nurse midwife for over twenty years. I was trained to view the minor and major discomforts of pregnancy to be hormonal or physiological in origin. It was not until I personally experienced three pregnancies and two births that I realized traditional midwifery and medicine did not have all the facts.

As a body-mind-spirit-energetic-healing practitioner, I specialize in energetically re-weaving fragmented parts of a person's spirit and soul to create a more centered and balanced human being. My unique gifts allow me to merge with any individual, at any given time and any location. During my own pregnancies, I was fortunate to have the ability to telepathically communicate with my unborn babies. The information my babies shared with me was so fascinating I was compelled to create *Birth, A Conscious Choice.*

I hope to give prospective parents and anyone else who reads this book a higher understanding about life. I hope to enlighten people about the necessary physiological and energetic changes that women make to facilitate the incredible process of pregnancy and birth. This book ventures into who we were before we came to this planet and the process that a baby has to undergo to become physical.

CHAPTER 2

▼

My pregnancies

After years of infertility, I finally became pregnant at the age of thirty-eight. Unfortunately, the pregnancy ended in a miscarriage when I was fourteen weeks pregnant. I was connected and deeply bonded to this little person growing inside of me. The loss of this pregnancy was devastating.

I meditated daily and traveled the universe with this little one. He called himself PP Penny. For six consecutive nights, he woke me up from a deep sleep, compelling me to put pen to paper. He dictated to me children's stories about animals and their feelings. This was a strange topic for me because I am not connected to animals. I was so blessed to have encountered PP Penny's brief physical form and for giving me a greater understanding about life.

On day three following the death of PP Penny, he came to me in a time of intense grief and spoke to me. He assured me I would have another child. He informed me he was leaving me even a greater gift and that was to experience grief at a cellular level. A strange gift, but as a healer it is important to resonate at a cellular level with the emotional issues of the client. For many years I had been a certified bereavement counselor for those experiencing pregnancy loss, but grief was about the only emotion I personally had never experienced.

Up until this point in my nursing career, I empathized and sympathized with many people going through the grief process. I had no idea that grief was more than an emotional state, but also a deep physical trauma to the body. A bond of love forms energetic cords from the center of our chest to the center of our loved one's chest. Death causes this love cord to tear and in doing so creates physical pain to the chest area. These tears within the love cords, if not handled and supported properly, will eventually create all sorts of emotional and physical constraints.

Following my miscarriage my biological clock was ticking. After all it took us 10 years to become pregnant with PP Penny. Knowing that I had only one fallopian tube due to previous pelvic surgery, the statistical chance of conceiving on my own was slim.

My husband and I decided to seek the assistance of an infertility specialist. Six months later after numerous doctor visits, lab tests, ultrasounds and sometimes taking four to six injections a day, I was removed from the *in vitro* fertilization program. Medically I was diagnosed with premature ovarian failure. In other words, I was in premature menopause.

I was told that the likelihood of ever becoming pregnant was zero, and if I wanted a child I should seriously consider adoption. Like many other couples that go through similar failed infertility treatments, this was another devastating moment within our relationship.

It would have been very easy to plunge into a state of despair and depression, but what good would that serve. I've always tried to see the higher picture in every scenario. My infertility experience gave me a higher understanding regarding the stress and the hardship some couples experience in their attempt to achieve a pregnancy. My heart goes out to all people who walked the path of infertility, and to say to you, never give up hope.

If you have a physical contract to be a parent, somehow or other this physical contract will manifest. The timing may not be as you desire, but when it happens, it will be the perfect time. God will orchestrate events in your life to facilitate the entry of that child. Today, reproductive endocrinologists have the technology to assist in this process. For success, however, it is your responsibility to heal unresolved emotional issues within your life. This in turn will allow you to become energetically open to pregnancy and the birth process.

Meanwhile, a very close friend of mine Elena was diagnosed with gastric cancer. As we both worked through her illness and dying process we often spoke about death and what it would entail. She promised to communicate with me after her death to let me know that all was well. Needless to say, she kept he promise. Out of the blue, I happened to meet a spiritual medium (someone who communicates with the deceased).

Elena spoke to me through the spiritual medium, letting me know she was doing very well and thanked me for all I did for her during her dying process. She described in detail the memorial gifts I purchased for her daughters. Elena had physically never seen or known about these pendants.

She also had an important message for me. She wanted me to mark a particular date in my calendar as a personal good news date. Elena repeated the date over and over again and insisted I write it down on a piece of paper. She was aware that I tend to forget dates as I live completely in the moment and have no concept of date or time.

Tears streaming down my face, I marked the date in my calendar. Deep inside myself I knew she was telling me the date of a baby coming in. I reckoned that if my intuition were wrong, the only other personal good news event for me would be winning the lottery.

I rushed home to review my menstrual calendar to see where Elena's predicted personal good news date would fall within my menstrual cycle. People with infertility issues become experts at calculating predicted dates of ovulation. My calculations indicated that I would be menstruating on Elena's personal good news date and therefore, there was no possibility of a pregnancy occurring. My menstrual cycle had been regular all my life, every 26 to 28 days without fail.

Miracles do happen. The month prior to Elena's predicted personal good news date, I had for the first time in my life two menstrual cycles within the same month. This put Elena's predicted personal good news date smack in the middle of my new menstrual cycle, and would be an optimum time for conception. I later found out that this date was also Elena's birthday. I did not win the lottery that day but instead my husband and myself had a very romantic evening. Walla! Nine months later our son Kyle was born.

Following the birth of our son Kyle the pressure was off as I felt so blessed to have a child. For months I found myself saying, "I cannot believe women do this a second time, never mind a third or fourth time". I was having a difficult time adjusting to my new role as a full time mother. It was for me much harder staying at home than working as a full time midwife.

When Kyle was about five months old I had this strange thought for about a week that I was contracted to have a second child. With my history of infertility, I had not considered having a second child as I was fulfilled with one child.

A month later, on my husband's birthday, I was awakened in the middle of the night with a very strong sexual desire. Every cell of my body wanted to mate with my husband. This was extremely unusual, as my sex drive was non-existent since Kyle was born. Needless to say we went with the hormonal flow and in the height of passion I had a strange thought that maybe I conceived. BINGO! Nine months later our second son Bryan was born.

CHAPTER 3

▼

Why we choose to come to this planet

This is the million-dollar question, as we come here for many reasons. The spiritual side of mankind will continue to exist even after death. The evolution of our spirit requires that we visit many planets prior to coming to Earth. Each place of existence has different aspects, different vibrational frequencies and different lessons to be learned.

This planet Earth is the only planet that has the full range of emotions, from being completely happy and content, to deep despair and depression, and everything else that lies in between. We will encounter many emotional and physical challenges during our experimental time here on this planet. Overcoming these challenges will facilitate our spiritual evolution.

Prior to our decent into the physical body we sat on a council with higher beings of light, and we were co-writers in scripting our life book. Now you may say, "I would never have written so much hardship or tragedy into my life." The truth is that you did. Without adversity we will not grow.

CHAPTER 4

▼

Who and what we were prior to conception

Looking at the bigger picture, our temporary assignment to this planet is a brief moment in time. In worlds beyond ours, there is no such thing as linear time. In spiritual language, we are ageless. Our human world needs a point of reference for both entry and exit and therefore the concept of age and time was developed.

For the majority of people, there needs to be a built in safety system to guarantee their correct exit date. We designed the physical vessel housing our great spiritual body to age and deteriorate. Others decide to exit quickly in the form of an accident or sudden death. Comparing both scenarios, it is easier for the departing spirit to exit quickly.

It is definitely more challenging and emotionally devastating for the dying person to be fully conscious that they are dying. Both however, serve their purpose to the spirit that is leaving and to those left behind.

Planet Earth is a very dense planet. The incoming spirit has to undergo a series of downloading exercises to accommodate it's descent into the mother's womb. For the majority of people, the download training exercise is received from many different lives on many different planets.

Most people have had prior interaction with planet Earth in what we commonly refer to as "a past life experience". This terminology should in fact be named a "previous emanation experience".

The word *emanation* refers to holding the position of a spiritual guide for other humans. Each and every one of us had prior planetary experience as a spiritual guide for other humans. As a spiritual guide for other humans we were assigned to assist, support, protect and mentor a particular person living the human experience.

Everything that the human in physical form experiences their assigned spiritual guide will also co-experience. Spiritual guides are not bound to time or space. They can co-exist in two or more places at the same time. Therefore, a spiritual guide can be guiding more than one human at any given time. This accounts for why some people consciously remember many different past lives (emanations) all around the same era.

Prior to our descent into the physical, we were assigned four spiritual guides who remain with us for the duration of our human experience. There is one exception to this rule. We can deliberately choose to have our guides changed. This is achieved through an authentic path of spiritual empowerment in which a person consciously chooses to become an "Adept".

Becoming an "Adept" has been one of the most spiritually profound energetic life-changing events that I have undertaken. The Adept initiatory process enables a person to become a stronger and a more protected human being. It increases a person's spiritual consciousness leading to a tenfold increase in their spiritual energy flow.

This planet needs higher-level initiates to assist in replacing fear with love and to help us move from separation to unity in a global attempt to ascend the human consciousness. To become a higher level initiate, one needs to contact an initiated Adept-Guide. They are located throughout the world and can be found by visiting: www.7thmysteryschool.com

Past unhealed emanation remembrances can be carried forward to this lifetime to be cleared. This accounts for the powerful healing that occurs with past life regression work. An example would be my personal remembrance of the spiritual revolution helping many women through the process of childbirth. In that time period there were no hospitals. Women delivered at home or in the fields. Many of these women lost their lives in the process from hemorrhaging or other complications.

This explains my passion to be a midwife in this lifetime. It also explains why, as a child, I had a fear of women dying in childbirth. Due to my prior spiritual experiences with childbirth, it made sense to find a career that I would be good at. Somewhere deep in my psyche, I had to make peace with the feelings that I had failed women in their time of need. I needed to prove to myself that childbirth is safe. I insisted in birthing both my sons at home surrounded by my parents and a few of my very close friends.

I had embraced the birthing process with open arms. I totally trusted my inner feelings that all would be well. I had total confidence in Lauren, my nurse midwife, whom I hired to oversee my safety. Needless to say, I did hemorrhage after the delivery of my second son as I was reliving prior unhealed spiritual scars. The only way I was going to heal this situation was to recreate the event and pass the challenge.

The truth is that we have never before been physical in this world. We would be crazy to even consider doing it a second time around. It is tough being human. For some of us, the downloading process into the physical was a very long procedure requiring a great deal of preparation. These people are commonly referred to as "old souls" because of their wisdom. For others, the process was very quick with little or no pre-training. These people almost always feel out of place in society and encounter greater challenges being in physical form.

In the bigger scheme of things it does not matter what spiritual lineage we descended from, whether it be Indigo, Angelic, Extra Terrestrial or so forth. The only thing that is important for us to know is that we are great spiritual beings having a human experience. Knowing our physical and spiritual lineage can help the process. It can bring a higher understanding into why we have certain behavioral patterns and why we choose certain career paths.

At a higher level of existence there is no such thing as race, skin color or ethnic background. We are all one, coming from the one creator God. Our prior planetary experiences coupled with our astrological blueprint will dictate our strengths and weaknesses. The book about our life was scripted to assist in the evolution of our spirit and to heal prior spiritual traumas. Clearing these spiritual traumas can be a major factor in clearing longstanding health issues, as was my case with healing myself from asthma and chronic fatigue syndrome.

Prior to our descent into the human form we viewed our planet and were saddened by it's state of disarray. We decided to take the challenge and come forth to do something about it. We observed that as the human ego came into power, we created a world of apathy, depression, anger, hate, blame, shame, guilt, control and rejection.

We agreed to take on a great deal of negative emotions for the purpose of experiencing and healing these emotions during our experimental time here as human beings. By clearing these negative emotions with elements of compassion, forgiveness and non-judgement, we make a tremendous stride in the evolution of our spirit. It also allows us to discover the divinity within ourselves.

We have a higher spiritual contract with many other humans that they will be healing the same issues at the same time. We end up having a physical friendship with some of them. As we heal together, we will heal humanity and raise the entire vibrational frequency of this planet.

CHAPTER 5

▼

Conception, a conscious choice

Deliberate, premeditated conscious choice to come to this planet can be a mouthful for some people to swallow. Each and every one of us consciously co-wrote and scripted the book of how our life would play out. We were quite particular whom we were going to cast to play each part. We deliberately choose our parents, family members, and all the major people we would encounter as we ventured throughout life.

On a higher level, we consulted with these major players to make sure they were up to the task. No matter what part in our life they were scripted to play, they had to keep their assigned parts. Some choose to be the parent, some the child, others the lover, the villain, the abuser and so forth. WOW! Some people within our lives have brilliantly played their parts.

To make life a bit more challenging and interesting, we scripted many scenarios that would or would may not happen, depending on the choices we made. Other scenes are destined to happen regardless of what we do or say. To make life less boring and more interesting, a great number of us scripted a great deal of drama within our life book. Now you may say, "why would I choose an abuser? Who in their right mind would choose to be sexually molested as a child?" Not unlike many of you I questioned many times what was I thinking when I decided to take on this human contract.

As an adult, I had my fair share of physical abuse and this was in hindsight, a great gift. It allowed me to have greater compassion for others that experienced similar violence within relationships. The truth is that people who hurt you the most in life are indeed your greatest teachers. These people actually do you great favors. At one point in my life I was completely non-accepting of this statement.

After many hours of therapy, I recognized the anger I was feeling towards certain people was in fact not directly related to that person at all. That particular person had the ability to push my anger buttons hard enough to force me to embrace and heal anger that was deep inside of me.

Please forgive me if I provoke a similar response within you. Welcome to the path of truth and healing. It is only through adversity that we heal and eventually encounter the divine within.

▼

CHAPTER 6

Single parent families and adoption

Nothing in life is accidental. Everything happens for a reason. We scripted our genetic lineage so that it would serve us in the highest possible way. Some of us required two active parental contracts. For others, the incoming spirit required one active parent who would be quite capable of giving us all that we need. Currently, the vibrational frequency of the children arriving into the planet today is so high that they do not require the full time attention of two parents.

Some beings choose to enter into a single parent situation or choose to enter a situation where their parents would eventually divorce. These children may adjust very easily to new family dynamics. They agree to enter into your family, and somewhere at a cellular level they are fully aware of the events that would transpire. Therefore there is no need for parents to worry about how their children will adjust when family dynamics change.

The best thing we can do for our children and ourselves when a marital relationship ends is to try to respect each other. Remember, if a divorce is unpleasant, you are building up future karma for yourself to clear. Children always get hurt when their parents fight. Never be vindictive. Honor the other person no matter what.

The more accepting you are of any situation, the easier it will be for everyone to move forward. Always remember that you wrote these major events in your life. Down the road you will be a better person for the experience. When one door closes, another will open.

Other spiritual beings desperately want to come to this planet and choose the family they wish to join. For some reasons the physical entrance into the chosen family may be impossible. These beings will set up a scenario where they enter into this physical world via a different set of parents.

Through the process of adoption they will end up in the correct pre-assigned family.

Adoption at a higher level is also pre-agreed upon. The bottom line is that the incoming child chooses both their biological and physical parents. The incoming spirit also chooses the precise scenario where conception would occur, whether it is through love, violence, under the influence of drugs or alcohol or within a medical laboratory. The child itself, along with its spiritual guides, divinely planned all incoming circumstances.

▼

CHAPTER 7

Miscarriage and terminations

Looking at the issues of spontaneous abortion, or termination of pregnancy, all events were pre-planned by the spirit prior to entry into this physical world. The incoming spirit is fully conscious of the social and medical background of the mother. Remember that the incoming spirit was a co-writer in scripting his or her life book in partnership with the two individuals that would facilitate conception. The spirit chooses the date and time of conception and death.

There is no such thing as an accidental death. Death occurs when our contracted time on this planet expires. Our exit plan will play out when God agrees with our spiritual body, our soul body and our physical body that it is time to depart. Recent changes in planetary energy have allowed some individuals to stay in physical form after their contracted exit date. This occurs when that individual agrees with God to take on a new spiritual contract and to serve humanity at a deeper level.

As mentioned earlier, one of the major reasons for any one of us coming into this physical world is to experience human emotions. Babies that choose to exit early in pregnancy fit into two categories. They may be very evolved spiritual beings who can master a huge array of human emotions within a few weeks or months. In this case there is no need for them to prolong their existence within this physical world.

The second category is the high vibrational beings that want to become physical but for some reason they need a trial run. Coming into physical form is a challenging event even for the spirit. Sometimes it takes more than one attempt. In such situations the spirit can reenter the mother, or perhaps someone else, at a later date.

Any pregnancy loss will cause emotional issues to surface and through the healing of these emotions the vibrational frequency of the individual increases. This is precisely what happened to me with my first pregnancy, referred to as PP Penny. He was such an evolved spirit that it was impossible for him to maintain his vibrational frequency to the density of my physical vessel. PP Penny recorded in his spiritual data bank all that was necessary to come into the physical. When the time was right he came back to me in the form of my son Kyle. In the interim I had numerous encounters with him on the astral plane.

In my midwifery career, I have seen hundreds of women carry intense guilt or grief over the loss or termination of a pregnancy. These unresolved emotional scars end up manifesting in all sorts of emotional and physical diseases. Mothers and fathers need to realize that everything is divinely planned and therefore, we should not consume ourselves with guilt.

The incoming spirit co-scripted it's life book. If the mother did not fulfill the scenario where the pregnancy was to end, then the spirit would find another situation to terminate the pregnancy. In the eyes of spirit, there is no such thing as right or wrong. There are no judgements. Everything is how it is supposed to be, plain and simple.

Grief is a real physical and emotional event. The sooner we get through it, the better it will be for all concerned. Prolonged grief not only holds us back in life, but it also holds back the deceased person.

Our unwillingness to let the deceased go prevents that person from doing what he or she needs to do in the afterlife. They need to be free to carry out their higher spiritual work. From their viewpoint, they are happy to be free of this very constricting shell that we call the human body.

Deceased people are no longer trapped in the physical vessel. They realize that they are vast, endless spiritual beings. They are now tapping into the greatness of which they are. They want to sing and dance with the angels. Our unwillingness to let them go inadvertently restricts their movement. The biggest gift you can offer a deceased person is to let them be free. They will always come visit you anytime you think of them.

I have helped numerous women and men clear themselves of pregnancy loss guilt and grief with the following simple ceremony. This ceremony should be done alone, allowing each individual to let go of his or her personal pain. In circumstances where there are other siblings involved, each parent should do their own individual ceremony followed by an additional family ceremony.

- Go out and purchase a small white candle.
- Sit quietly at home and light the candle.
- Think about the baby that died.
- Talk to the baby.
- Give your baby a name if you have not done so.
- Give thanks for the time you shared.
- Give your baby permission to disconnect from you.
- Give yourself permission to stop grieving or feeling guilty.
- Allow the candle to burn out on its own.

Purchase a small memorabilia to remind you of this wonderful person that touched your life. Some like a piece of jewelry. For others it may be a nice picture to hang on the wall. Some people choose to plant a tree or place a special ornament in the garden. Whatever works for you, go do it and be happy.

CHAPTER 8

▼

Infertility

It is a known fact that the number of couples undergoing infertility treatment is on the rise. There are many medical issues that result in infertility. Generally speaking, it is common these days for couples to put off having a baby until they are well settled in life with an established career and more mature in age. This age factor alone brings many challenges and risk factors.

Outside traditional medicine there is a whole area to be uncovered as to why people have a difficult time conceiving and carrying a pregnancy to a viable gestational age. This is called the energetic dynamics of the human body and the spirituality of pregnancy.

Traditional reproductive endocrinologists specializing in infertility have great knowledge of the human anatomy and the patterns of female hormones. They are experts within this field, however many of them lack the knowledge base when it comes to the energetic anatomy of the body and of the spiritual dynamics of pregnancy.

I feel strongly that if infertility specialists were to study and understand the energetic anatomy of the human body and the spiritual dynamics of pregnancy, their success rates would be higher. It would encourage them to embrace a holistic management plan for their clients.

After years of intensive study into the energetic dynamics of the human body, I now realize unsolved emotional issues play a major part in most medical conditions. Healing these emotional traumas can result in improved health, sometimes completely resolving the medical problem at hand.

No matter what our background is and no matter what efforts we make to become pregnant, the physical body has to have a positive energy flow to the pelvic area to sustain a viable pregnancy. Pelvic energy can be greatly increased by resolving family and relationship issues. A good healthy sexual relationship will also increase the flow of pelvic energy.

From the spiritual side of things, the incoming children onto this planet have a much greater vibrational frequency than ours. This can pose a real challenge for the incoming spirit and for the mother. The sooner the mother increases her basic vibrational frequency, the sooner she increases the possibility of conceiving and maintaining a pregnancy.

The mother can increase her vibrational frequency by walking the path of self-discovery and self-healing. It is imperative to let go as much as possible all unresolved emotional issues in your life prior to pregnancy. These issues can cause infertility and create a negative pregnancy outcome.

Alternative healing modalities cost money, but couples may spend thousands of dollars on infertility treatment plans with a significant failure rate. Couples can also increase the chances of becoming pregnant by approaching infertility with a holistic management plan that complements the traditional medical module.

Attempting to resolve the issue of infertility using a holistic management plan would include some of the following modalities, using spiritually conscious psychotherapists, energetic healers, homeopaths, reflexologist etc. Some healing modalities are more successful than others at quickly clearing unresolved emotional traumas and increasing your vibration frequency.

One of the quickest ways of increasing your vibrational frequency is to have your DNA activated. DNA (deoxyribonucleic acid) is an essential component of all living matter, present within the nucleus of each cell in the human body. The reason why it is important to have your DNA activated is that your DNA is the genetic blueprint of both your mother and father's DNA. All major traumas or medical issues that were encountered by either your mother or father, your grandparents and ancestors for seven generations are encoded within your personal DNA.

The process of activating the DNA is powerful at clearing the genetic negative encodement. The process allows an individual to hold more spiritual light in the physical body. More light results in raising a person's awareness, raising their vibrational frequency and raising their consciousness.

Light is intelligent energy. Light is unconditional love. Light is the source to all things. With increased light, a person becomes more empowered to achieve their heart's desire. This activation integrates light into areas of a person's DNA. To locate a *22 Strand DNA Activator* within your area visit: www.7thmysteryschool.com

CHAPTER 9

▼

Downloading into the mother's body

As stated before, the normal chain of events is where the incoming spirit sits in council with God, his or her spiritual guides, and the prospective parents. This so-called meeting can take place years in advance prior to pregnancy or it can be a last minute decision.

This can account for why some women have a very strong desire to become pregnant, and why they get so upset each month when a pregnancy has not occurred. It also accounts for why some psychics feel a strong presence of a child around women way before the physical manifestation of the pregnancy.

Somewhere within the psyche of the mother, she may have conscious contact with the being that is planning to come to her in the form of a child. This contact can be so profound that every cell of her body cries out to fulfill the contract. The incoming spirit has no concept of linear time, and will enter at the appropriate time. In the interim it connects with the mother and the bonding process commences.

For a period of time prior to the actual act of conception, the incoming spirit is separated from it's spiritual family in preparation for the human experience. (The truth is that the spirit is not actually separated, but it perceives that it is). The best way to try to explain the downloading process is as follows: The incoming spirit is placed alone in a room for a period of time as it acclimates to being alone. It can not have any contact with its spiritual family.

As time goes by, the spirit gradually forgets a great deal of information about it's former life. The new age term for this is being veiled from our totality of self. On the other hand, our spiritual family is constantly monitoring the spirit but can not have any contact, similar to a one way viewing wall within a police interview room.

No matter how prepared a spirit is for the downloading process nothing will make sense until experienced first hand. The isolation the spirit feels can be devastating. These traumas can be carried over into the emotional makeup of the human for processing and healing at a later date.

These emotions can range from anger towards God to feeling abandoned by their family. Some people go through life feeling alone, not fitting into society and non-accepting of their physical world. For the lucky ones, they are totally veiled from their previous existence and walk through life with ease.

At the moment of conception, the spirit is forced into the mother's body and envelops the fertilized egg. What a shock this can be for the spirit! One moment it was vast and boundless, and the next moment the physical body of the mother constricts it. This is in itself a huge core issue for many people. It also explains why some people have a huge need to control all situations or are afraid of being confined in small spaces.

CHAPTER 10

▼

The human energy system

The human energy system has it's own anatomical structure consisting of four bodies: The physical body, the aura, the soul body and the spiritual body. Billions of electrons and protons are found within the billions of atoms that merge together to create the physical body.

These electrons and protons are in constant motion and create an electrical magnetic field around the physical body called "the aura". The aura is in constant motion and emanates many colors depending on the emotional and spiritual state of the individual. The aura of a healthy person is strong, while the aura of an ill person will have a weaker feel.

Energetically sensitive people can pick up a great deal of information from all sorts of objects. The energetic vibration of the aura is transmitted to the objects that we have close contact with. For example, when a person is sitting on a chair for a period of time, the chair absorbs the auric energy of that person. The chair will probably feel slightly warm due to heat transfer and because it holds the energetic vibrational frequency of the previous person. The chair may feel uncomfortable to you if your auric energetic vibration is very different to that of the previous person's auric vibration.

Have you ever wondered why small children have a favorite blanket or soft toy? Due to the frequent handling of their favorite blanket or toy, the auric energetic vibrational frequency of the child is constantly infused into their special object. It is in total harmony with their emotional body.

Young children are pure love. Their favorite toy or blanket emanates that love and the object will feel very comforting to the child. A tired overstressed child will be balanced energetically every time he or she holds their favorite item. It is not uncommon for small children to be upset when their favorite blanket or soft toy is washed, as the washing process itself washes away the child's vibrational frequency.

The human aura extends up to 50 feet around the physical body. In a healthy person it is elliptical or egg shaped. The energetic feel or the vibrations of the aura vary from one individual to another. No two people are alike and no two people will ever have the same energetic constitution. Each of us has a unique vibrational frequency depending on our physical and spiritual lineage.

Individuals with similar auric patterns relate very well to one another. There can be an immediate bond that takes place at the very first meeting. People sometimes misinterpret this immediate connection as a past life (emanation) encounter.

On the other hand, individuals with a different auric pattern or auric colors may feel uncomfortable when first contact is made. There could be an immediate dislike or uncomfortable feeling between these people.

This does not mean that the other person is bad or has any issues to work out. It may however indicate that the two energy fields are not in harmony. There could also be an attraction to a person with completely opposite energetic patterns. The more we strengthen our aura and increase our spiritual awareness, the easier it is for us to immediately adjust to different auric patterns.

A 500-foot soul body surrounds the aura with the soul as the bridge between our physical body and our spiritual body. The soul is created at the moment we take our first breath of life and carries it's own vibrational frequency.

Prior to death, the soul begins to slowly loosen it's attachment to the physical body. This causes the aura to weaken and sometimes lose it's color. A very sick person may have a very dark and poor functioning aura. At the time of death, the soul will make a final disconnection from the physical body.

In addition to the soul body, an infinite spiritual body also surrounds us, which is our direct connection to our God source. It can expand anywhere within the universe but always remains directly connected to our soul body and our physical body. Our spiritual body allows us to telepathically communicate with people anywhere in the world. A body-mind-spirit-energetic-healing practitioner can expand his or her spiritual body anywhere within the world, therefore allowing them to perform long distance healing or readings.

Traditional medicine is excellent for treating disease at a physical level. Psychotherapists and psychologists are excellent at treating diseases at mental and emotional levels. Spiritual advisors support us with spiritual issues.

Chronic diseases can sometimes be difficult to cure. There are two reasons for this. The first reason is that the disease itself may one day be a catalyst in making you change your life. The second reason is you may not be healing the issue at the appropriate level within your human energy system.

Sometimes a disease penetrates all four levels of your being, the spirit, the soul, the aura and the physical. For example, you can have a physical ailment that originates at an emotional level within the aura. All the physical treatment in the world will only temporarily relieve the issue. The physical or emotional condition will continue to return in some form or other until that underlying emotional problem is resolved.

Should the underlying cause for your disease be spiritual in nature then it must be addressed at the spiritual, soul and aura level in order for the physical body to permanently heal. This may sound complicated, but there is a great deal of truth in saying that humans are complicated beings.

Reiki energy healing is one of the most common modalities available in the marketplace. I recommend that everyone do him or herself a huge favor and become Reiki attuned. Reiki (pronounced ray-key) is a Japanese technique for stress reduction and relaxation that promotes healing. Dr. Mikoa Usui discovered it in the early 1900's. It is a simple, yet powerful, technique that can be learned by anyone.

The word "Rei" means universal and "Key" means life force. This universal life force of energy needs to be turned on in order to have it flow. Developing babies and newborns love the energy of Reiki. I frequently used Reiki on my children during pregnancy and continue to do so as they experience childhood.

A Reiki master needs to physically turn on the flow of Reiki energy within your energy field. This process of turning on your healing energy is called a Reiki attunement. Almost every town in the USA have Reiki masters who are trained in the ancient art of Reiki.

Once you are Reiki attuned, you can turn on and off this Reiki healing energy as you please, for the rest of your life. When medical or emotional issues are chronic, you may want to seek professional assistance directly from energy healers who can reconstruct and realign major imbalances in a quick and productive manner. Once rebalanced, self-administered Reiki treatments will be more effective.

I also challenge you to walk outside the path of traditional medicine and seek professional assistance from holistic health practitioners. Like other body-mind-spirit-energy-healing practitioners, I am here changing one life at a time. A great many of us have walked the slow painful journey of self-healing. We are now coming out of the closet and saying, "there is a less painful way to walk this path, let us help!"

CHAPTER 11

▼

The chakra system

Special energy centers exist within the subtle bodies of the human energy system. These centers are referred to as "chakras" from the Sanskrit word meaning, "wheels". They resemble spinning vortices of subtle energies.

Our human energy system has seven major chakras accompanied with many minor chakras. The seven major chakras run from the base of the spine to the top of the head, supplying the body with life force energy. They play a major part in keeping all organs and bodily systems in good working order. In fact, we get more physical energy from our aura and chakra systems than from the food we eat.

The human experience can be quite challenging. On a daily basis we are exposed to various situations that overstress and overload our energy system. This can cause our chakra system to short circuit and as a result, we become unbalanced or ill.

The good news is that our aura and chakra systems can easily be tuned into higher vibrational states eliminating stress and promoting healing. Aura and chakra tune-ups can be achieved in a variety of ways. It can be as simple as finding ways to create relaxation and enjoyment in your life.

For more serious chronic states of imbalance within the body, one can practice meditation, yoga, martial arts, Reiki, etc. Any of the healing modalities that work directly on the energetic anatomy of the body will do wonders in creating and maintaining a state of balance and health.

Like all things within our universe, there are different grades of the same product and not surprisingly, energetic healing also comes in different amplifications. The level of healing an energetic healer transfers directly reflects the amount of personal issues he or she has processed, and what healing contracts the healer holds.

Essential oils are also a safe and effective method used for a multitude of medical and emotional conditions with successful results. Children respond very quickly to the aromas of these oils. There are many brands of essential oils on the market although the quality of oil can vary from one company to another. When choosing oils, please ensure they are Grade "A" oils. Should you need assistance with selecting essential oils for your medical condition, please visit: www.telephonehealing.com

Each chakra has a specific location, color and function. In a state of optimum health all chakras will work in harmony as one functioning unit. In the state of ill health, one malfunctioning chakra can affect the health of another chakra. I am going to give a very brief overview of the chakra locations and the medical conditions related to each chakra.

The 1ˢᵗ or Root Chakra

The first chakra is also called the "Root" chakra. The Root chakra extends downward in a cone shaped fashion from the perineum between the legs and into the ground. The color associated to the Root chakra is red. It supports the entire body. It directly feeds energy to the feet, legs, hip joints, base of spine, body bones, large intestine, sexual organs, immune system and the adrenal glands. Poor energy flow to the Root chakra may result in one or many of the following symptoms:

- Lack of physical energy
- Painful hip joints
- Hemorrhoids
- Varicose veins
- Obesity
- Bulimia
- Arthritis
- Lymphatic congestion
- Knee problems
- Low back pain
- Sciatica
- Rectal tumors
- Anorexia nervosa
- Constipation
- Immune deficiency
- Anemia

- Menopause problems
- Insecurity issues
- Issues with space boundaries
- Common addictions such as alcohol
- Inability to stand up for oneself
- A feeling that no place feels like home
- Unable to provide for life's necessities
- Exhaustion
- Issues with stability
- Issues with money

If after reading the above list, you feel that your Root chakra needs to be opened, here are some simple things you can try. The Root chakra vibrates with the color red. By wearing red on the lower part of your body, for example socks, underwear, pants, shoes or a full-length outfit, this chakra will open. This chakra also vibrates to the sound of the letter "O". Toning the sound "O" for about ten minutes each day will do wonders in keeping this chakra opened, and maybe relieve some of your health issues.

The 2nd or Sacral Chakra

The second or Sacral chakra is situated in the lower abdomen, about two or three fingers below the belly button. There are two parts to this charka, as they are shaped like ice cream cones, one flaring outward to the front and the other flaring outward towards the back.

The color associated with the Sacral chakra is orange. It directly feeds energy to the lower vertebrae, pelvis, appendix, bladder, genitals, kidneys, pelvis reproductive organs and the large intestine. Poor energy flow to the Sacral chakra may cause one or many of the following symptoms:

- Female reproductive health problems
- Male reproductive health problems
- Large intestinal problems
- Hormone imbalance
- Arthritis
- Unresolved blame or guilt
- Unresolved pregnancy issues
- Issues with intimacy
- Bladder trouble
- Lower back pain
- Appendicitis
- Control issues
- Financial problems
- Issues with empathy

- Unhappiness within a current relationship
- Issues with either giving or receiving
- Issues with emotions or feelings
- Addictions to sugar, food or alcohol

To facilitate healing of the Sacral chakra, wear the color orange on the lower half of the body as the sacral chakra vibrates to the color orange. This chakra vibrates to the sound "OO". Therefore to open this chakra, tone the sound "OO" for about 10 minutes every day and drink plenty of fluids.

The 3rd or Solar Plexus Chakra

The third or Solar Plexus chakra is located in the center of the body just under the diaphragm. It flares out to the surface of the body front and back like ice cream cones.

The color associated with the solar plexus chakra is yellow. It directly feeds energy to the stomach, liver, spleen, pancreas, gall bladder, kidneys, adrenals, small intestine and middle spine. Poor energy flow within the Solar Plexus chakra may cause one or many of the following symptoms:

- Abdominal gas and bloating
- Liver disease
- Gallbladder problems
- Diabetes
- Arthritis
- Colon or intestinal problems
- Lack of self-esteem
- Inability to trust others
- Having unnecessary fears
- Feeling of intimidation
- Resentment of caring for others
- Fear of making decisions
- Inability to assume responsibility for self
- Addictions to caffeine
- Indigestion
- Hepatitis
- Kidney problems
- Pancreatitis
- Gastric ulcer
- Skin problems
- Lack of self-respect
- Issues with power
- Issues with anger
- Issues with laughter

To facilitate healing of the Solar Plexus chakra, wear yellow on the upper half of the body as this chakra vibrates to the color yellow. This chakra also vibrates to the sound "AH". Therefore to open this chakra with sound, tone the sound "AH" for about ten minutes each day. Foods high in starch will comfort the solar plexus chakra.

The 4ᵗʰ or the Heart Chakra

The fourth chakra or the Heart chakra is located in the center of the chest between the shoulder blades and cones out in front and the back of the body. The colors associated with this charka are grass green or pink.

It directly feeds energy to the heart, lungs, cardiovascular, shoulders, arms, ribs, breasts, diaphragm, esophagus and the thymus gland. Poor energy flow within the heart chakra may cause one or many of the following symptoms:

- Allergies
- Heart conditions
- Breast cancer
- Asthma
- Arthritis
- Lung cancer

- Hypotension
- Shoulder problems
- Inability to give
- Inability to forgive
- Judgmental
- Addictions to nicotine or marijuana
- Upper back pain
- Bitterness
- Inability to receive love
- Demanding
- Resentment
- Self-centeredness

To facilitate healing of the Heart chakra, wear the colors green or pink that vibrate to this chakra on the upper half of the body. This chakra also vibrated to the sound of "Ay" as in play. Tone the sound 'Ay" for about ten minutes on a daily basis if you are suffering from any Heart chakra issues. An increase in dietary vegetables is a good way to assist in the opening of this chakra.

The 5ᵀʰ or Throat Chakra

The fifth or Throat chakra is located in the center of the throat and the base of the neck. It too, cones out in front and the back of the body. The color associated with it is light blue.

It directly feeds energy to the hypothalamus, parathyroid, gums, esophagus, thyroid, trachea, neck vertebrae, throat, mouth, teeth, ears, arms and hands. Poor energy flow to the Throat chakra may cause one or many of the following symptoms:

- TMJ (temporomandibular joint problems)
- Enlarged glands
- Chronic sore throats
- Thyroid problems
- Frequent colds or flu
- Recurrent fever blisters or oral herpes
- Inability to use personal power to manifest
- Fear of judgment and criticism
- Issues with personal expression
- Lack of faith and knowledge
- Inability to make decisions
- Unable to following one's dreams
- Unhappiness in one's profession
- Scoliosis
- Laryngitis
- Mouth ulcers
- Neck pain
- Gum disease

To facilitate healing of the Throat chakra, wear something in a nice blue color that vibrates with this chakra on the upper half of the body or around the neck. The sound "EE" as in see will also open this chakra. Therefore to open this chakra, tone the sound "EE" for about ten minutes each day. Eating plenty of fruit is valuable in assisting in the opening of this chakra.

The 6th Chakra or the Third Eye

The sixth chakra or the Third Eye is located in the center of the forehead. It cones out in front of the head at the center of the forehead and cones out from the back of the head at the nape of the neck, just above the hairline.

The color associated with it is sky blue or indigo. It directly feeds energy to the pineal gland, pituitary gland, brain, eyes, ears, nose and the nervous system. Poor energy flow within the Third Eye may cause one or many of the following symptoms:

- TMJ (temporomandibular joint problems)
- Brain tumors
- Swollen glands
- Thyroid problems
- Full spinal problems
- Neurological disturbances
- Headaches
- Fear of self-evaluation
- Hearing loss
- Fear of being open to new ideas
- Feelings of inadequacy
- Refusal to learn from life's experiences
- Stroke
- Hemorrhage
- Scoliosis
- Blindness
- Deafness
- Laryngitis
- Nightmares
- Eye problems
- Paranoia
- Anxiety
- Stuttering

To facilitate healing of the Third Eye, wear either sky blue or indigo blue on the upper part of the body, or around the neck. This chakra vibrates to the sound "MMM". Therefore toning the sound "MMM" will assist to heal issues related to this chakra.

The 7th or Crown Chakra

The Seventh Chakra or the Crown Chakra is located at the top of the head. It forms a single cone of energy going directly upward and out of the crown up into the sky. The colors associated with this chakra are violet, white and gold.

It directly feeds energy to the muscular system, nervous system, skeletal system, skin, central nervous system, cerebral cortex, the immune system and the pituitary gland. Poor energy flow to the Crown chakra may cause one or many of the following symptoms.

- Bone problems
- Chronic fatigue syndrome
- Multiple sclerosis
- Depression
- Lymphatic congestion
- Nervous system disease of any kind
- Muscle disease of any kind
- Cancer
- Arthritis
- Paralysis
- Obesity
- Insomnia
- Confusion
- Lack of faith

- ☯ Inability to see life's big picture
- ☯ Issues with attitudes
- ☯ Lack of inspiration
- ☯ Issues with values and ethics
- ☯ Issues with humanitarianism
- ☯ Lack of trust
- ☯ Lack of courage

To facilitate healing within the Crown chakra, wear violet, white and or gold anywhere on the body. Toning the sound "ing" for ten minutes every day will assist in healing issues within the Crown chakra.

CHAPTER 12

▼

The physiological and energetic dynamics of pregnancy

God certainly knew what he was doing when he chose women over men to have children. This is one thing men would be incapable of doing. If men were given this option, I think we would have very few children on this planet.

Pregnancy and birth are major events in a woman's life. No matter who we are or where we come from, we should have more respect, support and understanding for pregnant women, regardless of their social or financial background.

During pregnancy, every cell and every organ within the mother's body undergoes huge transformations to accommodate the needs of the growing baby. To maintain the huge oxygen and nutrient demand of a growing baby, the mother's heart increases in size.

By the time the mother is half way through her pregnancy, her cardiac output is increased by forty percent. This means that the mother's heart is pumping out forty percent more blood per minute. The mother's veins and arteries grow in length and diameter to accommodate this extra forty percent blood volume.

No wonder pregnant women get tired! This extra cardiac activity and blood volume alone are some of the major reasons why pregnant women are prone to developing palpitations, chest pain, high blood pressure, varicose veins and rectal hemorrhoids.

The average weight gain in pregnancy is approximately thirty-five pounds, gained over a seven-month period. Many women gain an excess of this amount. This weight gain can be very uncomfortable for the mother and when coupled with her growing uterus can restricts her physical movement. It is very frustrating to the mother to be unable to do some of the basic things in life like putting on her shoes.

The mother's liver and kidneys must also grow to accommodate this extra blood volume. The increase in renal activity results in the pregnant mother producing slightly more urine, another reason for the frequent bathroom trips. Extra kidney and liver excretions coupled with the increase in hormonal activity can cause the mother to develop itchy skin.

The mother's uterine muscles grow approximately three times in width and ten times in length to accommodate the size of the growing baby. This increase in the size of the mother's pelvic muscles can results in physical round ligament pelvic muscular pain. By the end of pregnancy, her stomach is so displaced under her lungs that she may encounter breathing difficulties.

Her bowels are additionally compressed with the growing uterus and can add to the development of hemorrhoids and sometimes constipation.

The mother's pancreas produces more insulin to balance the glucose requirement of the baby that can lead to pregnancy diabetes. Diabetics are classified as high-risk pregnancies and this can be emotionally and physically very stressful for the mother.

For years I managed high-risk pregnancies. I believed diabetes in pregnancy is one of the most challenging conditions the mother can face. We immediately instruct her to change her entire eating habits. On top of this we instruct her to analyze her blood sugar three to five times a day and conduct extra blood tests and ultrasounds. Her whole life changed when she discovered she was pregnant. The diagnoses of diabetes required an even greater life change.

The mother's entire sleep cycle is completely interrupted and it is not unusual for her to become sleep depraved. Every cell in the mother's brain is altered by pregnancy hormones, which can cause her to be forgetful. Hormonal levels are radically changed in order to sustain the pregnancy. Women are such incredible beings to facilitate this entire process.

An abdominal and pelvic energy shield created by the baby around the mother reduces the normal energy flow to the mother's stomach, bowel and pelvic region. This may result in heartburn, constipation and in some cases a decrease in her sexuality as the mother attempts to conserve her energy.

During pregnancy, the growing fetus and the growing uterus causes a distortion to the mother's sacral chakra, located just above the pubic bone. This in turn can either increase or decrease the mother's sexual desires. In the majority of cases, the mother makes the necessary energetic adjustments and pregnancy proceeds as normal.

For others, especially if her Sacral chakra is out of alignment prior to pregnancy, the mother may encounter more challenges and she may have a harder time sustaining the pregnancy. Should this occur, it would be advisable to seek the professional assistance of a body-mind-spirit-energetic-healing practitioner or a homeopath that may be able to strengthen your energy system to support both you and your baby.

The strange thing is that no matter what medical condition the mother develops, babies normally do very well. This is due to the incredible medical care available to women today, and the commitment mothers have to the well being of her baby. Modern medicine has saved many lives.

For mothers and babies who experience an unexpected bad pregnancy, there may have been other forces at play. The bigger picture is that all events and outcomes are preplanned. Babies sometimes choose to come into this world mentally or physically challenged. For whatever the reasons, we may never know.

I ask everyone who reads this book to increase your awareness of how challenging pregnancy and birth can be. The next time you encounter a pregnant woman, honor her and do whatever possible to make her life a little easier.

Up until I experienced my own pregnancies, I was always taught and believed that the minor and major discomforts of pregnancy were either hormonal or physiological in nature. I now know differently. Personally, I experienced three difficult pregnancies. I found myself swallowing every bit of advice that I ever gave other pregnant women in my twenty-year midwifery career.

Being spiritually conscious, I was fully aware that the children I was contracted to bring forward into this physical world were of an extremely high vibrational frequency. My personal challenge was to manifest them into this physical world.

From day one I stopped working. I was too dizzy and experienced heart palpitations due to the fact that I have a history of a common minor heart valve defect. Talk about a surrendering process! I went from a high-pressure career position to a high-risk pregnancy, literally flat on my back as my pregnancies took over.

I had no idea that pregnancy could be so difficult. Many times I would sit on my bed thinking I was going to die. I was so weak from vomiting and not eating adequately that it was difficult to find the joy of pregnancy that so many people talk about. I felt I was being pushed back in my body as the baby took over. The only thing I could do was be a witness and experience the event.

I was aware how every cell and energy center in my body was changing. I developed a higher understanding as to why some women experience moderate to severe nausea and vomiting in pregnancy. Yes, it can be partly due to hormonal levels.

Looking at the bigger picture, it is also partially due to the fact that the energy makeup or feel, of the incoming spirit is different from that of the mother's. This lack of harmony between the mothers, and the baby's energetic patterns can literally make the mother physically sick.

It could be likened to this analogy. Think of someone that makes you uncomfortable when they are in your presence. Now put that person inside your body twenty-four hours a day for a few months and imagine what it would feel like. No wonder pregnant women feel sick!

On the other hand, some women have greater compatibility with the incoming spirit and for them, pregnancy is easier to handle. It may take a few months however for the mother's energetic system to make the necessary adjustments to pregnancy.

I am constantly amazed at how incredible women are. Not only do they have to accommodate the physical growth of the baby, but also accommodate the permanent attachment of the incoming baby's spiritual body to her body. Very early in pregnancy the incoming baby forms a protective energy shield all around the mother's abdomen and pelvic region.

All words and thoughts about a person are released from the sender in the form of energy. A good thought feels gentle and supportive to the recipient. On the other hand, a negative thought or a mean gesture to a person creates uncomfortable sharp shaped energetic structures that form in the energy field of the recipient.

These sharp shapes energetic structures can be very damaging to the baby and to the ability of the mother to sustain the pregnancy. It is amazing that the baby knows how to protect itself from these negative forces.

Some pregnant women become upset when people touch their abdomens. Never reach out to touch a mother's pregnant belly without asking for permission. Your energetic constitution may be different from that of the incoming baby, and it is a mother's natural instinct to protect her offspring. Question the mother how she feels when people touch her belly. Her answer will tell you if it is something she likes or dislikes.

This incoming spirit has it's own life history and issues to resolve during it's stay here on this planet. The more spiritually conscious the mother is, the more she has the ability to pick up some of this information from her baby. I was amazed at all the emotions my own children had carried within their cells as a direct result of the downloading process. I did a great deal of emotional release work on my babies when they were still in my uterus.

For most of us, it was inappropriate to express negative emotions as children. The children on this planet at the present moment are very emotional and environmental sensitive beings. They constantly filter emotions through their bodies and are great at releasing them in the moment. Because of their sensitivity to everything that goes on around them, it is not unusual for their systems to become overloaded.

This world would be a different place today if parents had the knowledge of how to energetically clear their children of excess emotions. Once again, the word Reiki comes up, as it is one of the simplest ways to clear our children.

Towards the very end of pregnancy, the spiritual guides assigned to the incoming baby are more active in the energy field of the mother. This increase in activity can be unsettling for the mother, and it is not unusual for pregnant women to be a little restless towards the end of pregnancy.

It is also not unusual for the pregnant woman to become more spiritual and psychic during pregnancy. Pregnancy is a sacred act, fulfilling the entry of incredible spiritual beings onto our planet.

Women who are willing to experience the sacredness of pregnancy allow themselves to tap into their own greatness and divinity. The bliss that I felt as I energetically connected with my own babies during pregnancy is impossible to describe. It was a special sacred encounter that only a mother can understand.

CHAPTER 13

▼

The incredible process of birth

Birth is an amazing process. Many events are happening at the same time. For starters, there has to be great harmony between the mother and baby for this process to proceed normally. As previously discussed, the exact time and place of birth are pre-planned. The birth time is crucial and it is a well-known fact that astrology has an important part to play in the destiny of a person.

The incoming spirit will set up scenarios to facilitate the correct birth time. The mode of delivery and all labor scenarios play out as they were planned. Under normal circumstances of labor, during each contraction, the baby feels intermittent intense squeezing of his or her entire body.

Just imagine been surrounded by a very large rubber balloon with little or no room to move. This is what it is like for a baby *in utero* at the end of pregnancy. Suddenly and without warning, the balloon around you squeezes very tightly, a frightening and uncomfortable experience. The process happens over and over as labor intensifies, causing uncertainty, fear and pain to the baby.

It is imperative for the mother to send thoughts of reassurance to her baby during labor and delivery. In your mind, talk to your baby. Explain that labor has started and that this is a temporary process. Constantly reassure your little one that he or she is safe.

Not only does the baby have to put up with the pressure of the contractions, it has to change the size and shape of it's head to accommodate the size of the mother's pelvis. This alteration in the size and shape of the baby's head is part of normal labor and is known as molding (when the bones of the skull overlap each other). Excessive molding leads to a baby having a temporary cone shaped head, which can cause headaches for the baby.

It is not uncommon for the baby to experience a reduction in his or her oxygen supply as the umbilical cord is compressed during contractions. Last but not least, the baby has to twist and turn his or her neck into very uncomfortable postures to descend down through the birth canal.

No matter what attempts the parents make for a gentler birthing process, under normal circumstances, babies experience uncertainty, fear and pain during birth. Today it is more common for births to be medically managed which can lead to more physical and mental stress for these little babies.

As the baby is doing his or her own thing, the mother has to amplify her hormonal production. She has to facilitate good regular contractions lasting at least sixty seconds, moderate to strong in intensity, and repeat the process over and over again until the baby is delivered. They do not call childbirth "labor" for no reason, as it is indeed intense physical work for both the mother and baby.

The onset time of labor is unpredictable, however many women start labor at the end of a busy workday. The mother is often tired and has to face a rough twelve to twenty four hours of labor. During labor, every organ in the mother's body slows down, as her uterus takes over for the biggest marathon it has ever experienced.

It is the most amazing thing to experience your uterus taking complete control of your entire body. One moment you are walking and talking and the next moment you are drawn to your knees unable to move. You breathe for your dear life to get through the pain, as every muscle in your uterus contracts as hard as it can. Each contraction causes the uterus to shrink in size to push the baby down and out through the pelvic canal.

The outcome of labor is determined by all the above factors plus the size and shape of the mother's pelvis. There is no hard and fast rule on how well the mother's pelvis will open during labor until it is put to the test. There is no accurate way of measuring the mother's pelvis in pregnancy except for x-rays, and this is not preferred due to the potential danger to the baby.

The ongoing hormonal changes within the mother allow the bones of her pelvis to open up to a certain degree in late pregnancy. The labor process itself will further open the pelvis. The pressure from the baby's head pushing down into the mother's pelvis as labor is in progress can sometimes cause severe back and pubic pain. I recommend for new mothers to have pelvic chiropractic adjustments as soon as possible after childbirth to realign the pelvic bones.

Once the baby's head has entered the pelvis during the last few weeks of pregnancy, it is impossible to take x-ray measurements because the baby's head is in the way. Just because a baby's head fits into the mother's pelvis does not mean it will come out of the pelvis. There are many small sections to the pelvis, and if any one of these points is more prominent than normal, it can prevent the head from rotating down into and out of the pelvis.

There are four different types of pelvises: The gynecoid, the anthropoid, the android, and the platypelloid. The preferred pelvic type for childbirth is the gynecoid pelvis, commonly referred to as the "female pelvis" and is present in approximately forty percent of women.

The second pelvic type is the anthropoid pelvis. It occurs in approximately twenty five to forty percent of women. This pelvis type is adequate for childbirth, but favors the baby's head entering the mothers pelvis with it's face pointing towards the mothers pubic bone thus creating a longer labor.

The third pelvic type is the android pelvis, sometimes referred to as the "male pelvis" because it is heavier and can be a problem for the mother. This male pelvis is seen in approximately fifteen to thirty percent of women. It has more prominent bony structures, and can cause the baby to get stuck, as the head tries to turn within the pelvis to accommodate the birth canal. Overall, it results in a longer labor and increases the chance for an instrumental delivery or a Cesarean Section birth.

Last is the platypelloid pelvis, which occurs in three percent of all women and is not at all conducive to a vaginal birth. The incidence of Cesarean Section births is on the rise, looking at this data helps explain why cesarean section births are necessary, however there are a lot of unnecessary cesarean sections performed.

For my own deliveries, I rented a birthing pool and set it up in my living room as soon as labor started. Relaxing in warm water is a wonderfully safe method of pain relief during labor, and it is a very gentle way to birth your baby.

My first labor lasted fourteen hours with intense contractions, much like the personality of my son, Kyle. At times when I was in the full force of labor with Kyle, I found myself thinking of all the women I had coached either in labor or during my Lamaze classes on breathing techniques. It was a whole different experience when the Lamaze breathing was accompanied with contraction pains.

I could not believe labor was so painful. I did not use any pain relieving drugs because I chose to have a home birth. During my first labor my cervix opened nicely to seven centimeters but those last three centimeters took hours.

I will admit at one stage I was on my hands and knees in the shower, pleading for drugs. It was a good job I had a wonderful encouraging labor support team, each and every one of them playing an incredible part in my sons birth being orchestrated in front of them.

My husband John, was my pillar of strength for my entire pregnancy and birth. My girlfriend Debra, who is also a wonderful midwife, allowed me to embrace the power and force of labor with confidence and letting go of all inhibitions about being naked in front of my labor team.

My friend Lucy did a perfect job attending to all my physical needs for hours as she wiped my brow and provided me with everything I needed. My friend Joan was my photographer and just having her present as I birthed was a great comfort to me.

My friend Sue, who is a great energy healer herself, held the divine mother energy for me throughout the whole process. She would look me directly in the eyes and transferred her strength to me.

During my entire labor my mother sat quietly in the room praying that I would get through labor quickly and safely. She was wonderful helping wherever she could. My poor father sat in the kitchen for over fourteen hours, boiling water for the birthing pool and making tea for everyone.

It must have been very difficult for my parents to hear their daughter cry out in labor. I have five brothers and two sisters and this was the first time my father had heard a woman in labor. In my mother's time, the woman was isolated in the labor ward while the husband remained in the waiting room or told to go home.

I will be forever grateful to all my birth buddies, and to spirit for orchestrating a series of events that lead me to meeting my midwife Lauren. I could not have asked for a better midwife. Not only is Lauren brilliant playing her midwifery role, but she is also an incredible spiritually conscious person. I felt so safe with her.

Thank God for the courage of midwives like Lauren, and their back up physicians who give women the option of home births. This is indeed a very special gift to both the incoming spirit and their families.

A hospital managed birth would have required me to use the medication called Pitocin to enhance uterine contractions. I knew if I did not progress, I would be transferred to a hospital. The position of my baby was not helping as he was directly occipital posterior, meaning delivering face up instead of down.

After hours of steady labor with no progress, I decided to seek the assistance of two powerful energy healers named Laurie and Gudni, whom I received a great deal of my spiritual training from. I telephoned them and explained my situation. I was determined to have my baby at home.

Laurie and Gudni immediately worked on me to facilitate cervical dilation. The irony is I used their expertise earlier in this pregnancy to facilitate cervical closure when I was twenty-five weeks pregnant in pre term labor. In my heart I knew if it were not for the assistance I received from these wonderful energy healers, and for my midwife Lauren's birth management, I would have been transferred to the hospital and delivered by Cesarean Section.

Following my first delivery I scheduled a Lomi Lomi massage to assist my body in recuperating from the birthing process. A Lomi Lomi massage is a sacred and spiritual form of massage and is truly something to be experienced. It automatically elevates a person to a higher state of consciousness. As soon as I relaxed on the massage table I experienced my birth all over again from a spiritual viewpoint.

At the time of the actual birth, I pushed for about two hours and was completely focused on the physical side of the whole process. All women will agree that birth is a truly physical process. By re-entering the birth scene of my son Kyle, I was shocked at how many non-physical beings were present in my home at the time of his birth.

Deceased relatives and friends gather around a birth scene to give us spiritual strength and support. Spiritual guides, belonging to the mother and the baby, are also present. My bedroom was so jammed packed that they were waiting out in the hallway!

Suddenly, I entered the consciousness of my baby as he made his final descent through my pelvis. In that few minutes just prior to his birth he became terrified, unable to breathe, as his umbilical cord was relatively short and wrapped tightly around his neck. In that moment he felt so alone and isolated. He feared death and not being able to make it into this physical world. Then suddenly his neck was twisted into a very difficult position to accommodate the shape of my pelvis and that caused him to experience severe neck pain.

At the moment of Kyle's birth, he found himself in a confusing situation. He went from being violently squeezed by my uterus and pelvis, to being free of all physical pressure. He could not comprehend what happened. He had survived the birth process and was now **HUMAN**.

At the moment of his first breath, his soul was infused between his spiritual and physical body. What a remarkable process this is! Our soul is infused into us at the time of the first breath of life. Thank God for a little oxygen sometimes necessary to allow these little ones to get over the shock of birth.

The above insights into what each baby experiences at the time of birth makes me even more determined to encourage parents and family members to be active participants in the birthing process. I urge people to cuddle and nurture their newborn as soon as possible and for as long as possible after birth.

Hospital staff will care for your baby but this is simply work for them. Your baby is no more special than the baby in the next crib. You and your family members have bonded with your baby and are the best people to give the baby the emotional support he or she requires.

As soon as possible after birth, lavish your baby with love and reassurance. Explain to your little one that he or she has just survived the process of birth and it is normal to have some physical pain. Tell your little one you are here to take care of all his or her needs.

Communicate with your baby and ask that they are receptive to having their energetic body, soul body and spiritual body easily and effortlessly merge with yours. Ask your baby to be receptive to developing a harmonious relationship with you. Welcome this incredible spiritual being, masked within this tiny little body, into your world. Always explain to your baby what to expect over the coming weeks and months.

These instructions may seem odd but if you follow them, it is more likely that you and your baby will have a much easier post partum transition phase. Remember to pass on these welcoming instructions to your partner or labor coach in case you have complications and for some reason you are not the first one to physically communicate with your baby.

My second labor was an altogether different experience. I labored all alone, sending my husband and parents to bed, thinking that they may be up all night. I meditated for about five hours as I experienced regular painless contractions. I was waiting for the full force of labor to completely consume my body as the first labor did. I felt this was too easy to be true. Something told me that I had better wake my husband and parents to set up the birthing pool in case I needed it.

Without warning I was fully dilated which means I was ready to push the baby out. It was almost comical. I went from a state of meditation to a state of urgency on the phone calling my midwife and my two dear friends who were planning to be at the birth to come over as soon a possible.

I was in a state of panic when my friend Joan arrived. I was squatting in the birthing pool, trying not to push. I was so relieved to see her, not just because she is my friend, but she is also a nurse with years of intensive care nursing experience. This was reassuring to me, as my biggest fear in any birth, is delivering a baby that requires resuscitation.

Joan was wonderful as she rolled up her sleeves and was ready to assist birthing my baby if my midwife did not arrive in time. This took a great deal of pressure off my husband and parents. I remember Joan looking at me directly in the eyes and telepathically conveying to me that everything would be fine.

In that moment of direct eye contact she empowered me and I felt very reassured and comforted. I remembered asking Joan what I should do and she answered "breathe". What a powerful word to use when someone is in deep distress. I was so consumed with the pain and force of labor I was forgetting to breathe.

Soon my friend Sue arrived and right behind her was my midwife Lauren and her assistant. Two pushes later my son Bryan was delivered under water in a directly posterior position with his face facing upwards. He has a calmer personality. Women often associate their labor patterns to the personality traits of their children. There may be a great deal of truth to this.

I had a massive hemorrhage an hour or so following the birth of Bryan, loosing almost half of my total blood volume. The hemorrhage was not obvious because I was forming blood clots within my uterus. I wanted to pass urine so badly and being the stubborn person I am, insisted on getting up to go the bathroom.

Needless to say, I passed out as I sat on the toilet. As I energetically and spiritually looked back into this incident, I could hear the angels say, "her vitals are dropping, we are losing her". I now realize I was contracted to die during this delivery.

The only thing I can consciously remember about this incident was feeling I was passing out. I could hear my midwife Lauren and friends asking me if I could hear them. I kept saying "yes I can hear you but not see you". This was followed by a period of time where I have no recollection of what happened.

My friend Joan heard all the commotion going on in the bathroom and ran down to see what was happening. To her amazement she was frozen in her tracks, as if an energetic wall was placed in front of her preventing entrance into the bathroom. This was a deliberate action by my spiritual guides.

On a higher spiritual plane my time had expired and I was planning to depart from this physical world. I did not want to be resuscitated as I had accomplished what I came here to do, bringing two great spiritual beings into this physical world. I had no fear of death.

I absolutely know that the human experience is temporary and one of the hardest things we have to experience in the evolution of our Spirit. I will celebrate my exit moment, as it will once again allow me to have full union with my angelic brothers and sisters and God himself. At a higher level I knew everything would work out fine for all concerned. During this brief moment of no longer being in the physical, I was shown the ramifications of what my decision to die would be.

I was shown the emotional challenges my children would have without a mother. Although my husband would be quite capable of raising the boys on his own, it would be difficult for him. He would have to place them in day care and this would not be in the highest and best interest of our children. I was shown the grief my husband, my parents, my friends and my midwife would suffer if I choose to leave. I was also shown the bad publicity home birthing midwives would get.

My friend Sue traveled to the astral plane with me in my moment of choice. Sue and I have traveled the path of self-discovery for years together, and we are deeply connected to each other. I value her opinion and support a great deal.

She knew that I had not just passed out, but I was traveling on the astral plane and might not be returning. She forcefully commanded me to return to the physical. I obviously listened to Sue's advice and came back.

In choosing to return, I was assigned a higher spiritual contract of being a world healer performing "Soul Reweaving's" at event's called TIME TO HEAL. I was instructed to bring large groups of people together for these events.

During my TIME TO HEAL events I will energetically view the condition of large groups of Souls in a manner similar to that of inspecting a delicately crocheted baby's blanket. I will scans for broken threads, tears and discoloration's. I will then energetically repair and reweave the damaged areas. Intense light is fused into the discoloration's recharging that section.

These events are designed to facilitate massive emotional healing for all those attending and hopefully will be a major turning point for participants to find and follow their life passion. The Soul has always been the bridge between our physical and spiritual bodies. A Soul Reweave facilitates clearer communication between the spiritual body and the physical body resulting in a higher consciousness.

CHAPTER 14

▼

Why post partum can be challenging

Personally, I found the post partum period (the first six to eight weeks following childbirth) to be the most challenging part of the entire process of having a baby. There is so much focus and information out there about pregnancy and labor, and relatively little spoken about the post partum period. With my first son, I can remember that on the third day following birth I was crying on the telephone with my sisters in Ireland and my close friends. I was feeling very emotional and inadequate.

The rapid decrease in hormones that occurs approximately on the third, the fifth and the tenth day following birth can be emotionally challenging for the mother. These are the days when the mother may cry for no apparent reason. Nothing you can say or do will make her feel better.

The best thing you can do to prevent new mothers from being over stressed is to honor her wishes. Initially, the art of breast-feeding can be very awkward for the new mother. She should be able to sit comfortably anywhere within her own home without worrying about what she is wearing or how she is looking.

It is inconvenient for nursing mothers to have to isolate themselves every time they wish to nurse their baby for fear of embarrassing friends or family members. It is a good idea for relatives and friends to make a telephone call to the new mother prior to visiting.

The emotional and energetic adjustments the mother makes post partum can consume most of her energy. She is also more sleep deprived than ever. Do not get upset if the telephone answering machine is on. It takes a lot of energy to talk on the phone with someone, and yet we do it all the time.

In the later part of pregnancy it is a good idea to discuss with your relatives your immediate post partum plans regarding visitations. Grandparents and family members will be very excited to visit the new arrival to the family. In the ideal world it would be great to have total harmony with our parents and in-laws, but unfortunately this is not always the situation.

To avoid embarrassing or uncomfortable situations, give a copy of this book to your relatives and maybe they will be more open and understanding regarding your wishes. Relatives need to put their personal preferences aside and focus on how they can best serve this new family. A happy and contented mother and father means a happy baby.

With my first son I was very exhausted for the first few days following birth. My physical body was a wreck. I honestly felt like I had been run over by a truck as every cell in my body hurt. I found myself comparing myself to my younger sisters. I thought they adjusted very well following childbirth. It was only because I am so brutally honest with people that they all let me in on their secrets.

They confirmed that the post partum period could be an extremely difficult time following the birth of a baby. Their personal experiences were not unlike mine, but for the most part they successfully hide their feelings. Most women feel that society has a high expectation of them as a new mother. It is expected that a new mother is grateful for this beautiful baby she has brought into this world. According to society, new mothers should be elated and full of joy with a newborn baby.

Personally with my first baby, I thought I might die. On the third day following birth my blood pressure suddenly elevated and I put on ten pounds of fluid overnight. I remember looking in the mirror and did not recognize myself. At forty-one years of age I was in bad shape and too stubborn to call my midwife to let her know how I was actually feeling. Having a baby literally brings you to your knees in surrendering and hopefully allows us to enter a state of gratitude. With my first birth the only thing I was grateful for was being alive.

I was even more surprised that I did not have the physical energy to bathe my baby myself. I had unrealistic expectations that I would be the most active person attending to my entire baby's needs. I had bathed and cared for hundreds of newborns in my midwifery career, so it was only natural for me to care for my own baby.

My physical exhaustion rendered me incapable of doing everything myself. I was so grateful for the fact that my husband, my mother and father were there to help me. It was enough for me to care for myself and breast-feed the baby. I could not have imagined what it would have been like if I did not have my support system in place. I advise all women to have a support person lined up (to assist with cooking and cleaning for you) for at least the first week post partum.

I was wiser for the second time around. Within twelve hours of delivering my son Bryan, I was at the chiropractor office. I went three subsequent days in a row. I had my pelvis, hips and back adjusted back into their normal positions, which made a huge difference in my recovery. I recommend chiropractic pelvic adjustments to all women as soon as possible after childbirth. Vaginal birth distorts the body and a chiropractor is trained to realign the bony structures.

My heart goes out to the women who have Cesarean Section births. Not only do these women have to make normal post partum adjustments, but also they have to recover from major surgery. We sometimes forget that a Cesarean Section birth is major surgery and needs recovery time. We as health care providers or as family support persons should be more generous in supporting mothers in their recovery process. All too often the mother's needs are forgotten as everyone focuses on the newborn.

Within the first twenty four to forty eight hours following childbirth, the mother's body undergoes rapid physiological and energetic changes. Her kidneys are put into maximum output mode as she excretes the extra fluid volume that was required during pregnancy.

This can sometimes overload the mother's circulatory system. Some women develop bad swelling, especially of the legs, which can be quite painful. The increased kidney activity causes the mother to urinate frequently and this can be uncomfortable on top of fresh stitches on the perineum, if an episiotomy was performed.

It is not unusual for a post partum mother to be tired as most women after labor are running on sleep depravation. She will experience a heavier vaginal blood flow than any previous menstrual period, which can be very exhausting. It is important for post partum mothers to have a good protein intake to maintain high energy.

One of the most useful gifts you can give a post partum mother is a gift of food. Find the name of a tasty take out restaurant within her town that has a delivery service. She will send you many blessings when she uses your gift certificate.

The physical body takes four to six weeks to return to its pre-pregnant state. I deliberately use the word physical body. It can sometimes take months for a woman's emotional, mental and sexual energy to return to the levels they were prior to pregnancy.

CHAPTER 15

▼

Breast-feeding

I am a strong supporter of breast-feeding as it has so many benefits for the baby. Throughout my midwifery career, I have assisted many mothers in successfully breast-feeding their babies. All babies are different and all have a different sucking pattern. Like many others, I also said to new mothers, "it only hurts when the baby initially latches onto the nipple, but then it gets better". It was not until I experienced breast-feeding myself that I can say that for some women "IT HURTS".

Breast-feeding is supposed to be a natural process. Sometimes we make ourselves feel guilty if we cannot successfully breast-feed our babies. I was not prepared for the physical and emotional drain I experienced while breast-feeding. My personal breast-feeding challenges humbled me. I never considered bottle-feeding my baby as I assumed I would naturally breast-feed. Being Irish, my skin is on the fair side. Within a few days of breast-feeding I had cracked nipples and within a week developed an infection in my left breast. I was a mess both physically and emotionally.

I wanted to give my baby a good start in life so I frequently spoke to a lactation consultant for support. I was determined to persevere as everyone kept telling me it would get easier. It never did get easier. In fact, every time I put the baby on the left breast I would experience a severe sharp nerve pain radiating from my left nipple going all the way to my back. It was torture, but I hung in there for five weeks. After all, breast is best.

I did not experience any joy from breast-feeding. The reason why I stopped breast-feeding was not because of the physical torture I was experiencing, but the negative emotional thoughts I was having. I started to hate breast-feeding and I feared my son might pick up my negative feelings. I stopped cold turkey and my baby had no adjustment issues. He loved the bottle and went from feeding every two to three hours to every four hours, which gave me rest I desperately needed.

However, I was not prepared for the subsequent two weeks of torture I experienced from permanently engorged breasts. In all my years of midwifery, I never had any woman come to me and complain about the pain that they experienced upon discontinuing breast-feeding. For almost two weeks I could not sleep on my side and it was agony getting out of the bed due to breast pain. It was also uncomfortable to hold my baby as every muscle and nerve in my breasts hurt.

In fact, I was so turned off breast-feeding that I refused to breast feed my second son. I can remember my midwife Lauren trying to talk me into breast-feeding, but I did not want to discuss the issue. I bottle-fed my second son Bryan for three days. What a blessing it was to have formula.

On day three my breasts became so engorged and I felt guilty that I did not give him a chance on the breast. Well the next moment I was fully breast-feeding him with the assistance of a nipple shield as it was too painful to put him directly onto the nipple. To my amazement I ended up fully breast-feeding him for seven weeks.

For avid supporters of breast-feeding you may be disappointed that I give such negative comments. I am sharing my story not to turn women off breast-feeding, as for millions of women it is a wonderful experience. I am sharing my story in order to address the possibilities of encountering breast-feeding challenges and to let women know that if breast-feeding does not work out as planned, they have not failed.

CHAPTER 16

▼

Bonding

The bonding that occurs during pregnancy is different from the post partum baby bonding. Some women fall madly in love with their newborn at the moment of birth. For others, this immediate love connection may not happen immediately after birth, but may take weeks or months to develop. The concept of falling totally in love with your baby from the moment he or she is born is a concept and not a reality for many women.

Society gives us the image that there is no greater love than the love between a mother and her newborn baby. I am here to say this is not the case for all women. There is nothing wrong with the woman who has a difficult time bonding.

The energetic dynamics of each pregnancy and the post partum adjustments are different for each woman. The newborn baby may have a very different energy pattern than that of the mothers. It may take weeks or even months for both energies to synchronize. This lack of synchronicity between the mother and baby can create an extremely stressed post partum period for the mother and a very fussy baby.

Babies do not enter this physical world knowing all the ins and outs of how to make the necessary adjustments to being in this physical world. Sometimes, the great spirits within their tiny physical bodies have a difficult transition phase as well.

After trying all the normal physical and emotional ways of comforting your baby and if he or she is still unsettled, then it is time to get help. Seek the professional assistance of a body-mind-spirit-energetic healing practitioner that has the ability to work on both you and your baby over the telephone, for a long distance healing session. Babies are very sensitive to the parent's emotions, therefore the more centered and balanced you are, the more centered and balanced your baby will be.

I have deliberately not mentioned the important role the father has to play in the bringing of a child into this world. The reason for this is that many women go through pregnancy alone with no support from the birth father. For these babies, the role of the birth father is strictly that of providing his sperm for conception to take place.

The bigger picture is that the mother will be capable of providing the child's entire needs. I have a great deal of honor for single parents as it is not an easy task raising a child, even when there is an active two parent contract in place.

For the millions of babies that choose to come into this world where both parents are actively involved in parenting the child, then the birth father becomes a very important part of the whole birth process. These babies need to be bonded with both parents. The father's role throughout pregnancy and birth is that of being supportive to both the mother and baby.

The father should do whatever is humanly possible to create an environment of peace and harmony within the home for the mother. The more he understands and supports the mother, the easier her pregnancy will be. Fathers should be willing to do extra chores around the home to conserve the mother's energy.

The energy of love is critical in creating a state of health and balance for both the mother and baby. The more love you show towards the mother and baby, the healthier your baby will grow. The mother is a human incubator, feeding and nurturing this incredible being which is growing inside her body.

Mothers who have more than one child will admit that their love bond with each child is different. Their relationship with each child is also different. In my first pregnancy I was bonded and connected right from the start. As stated before, I meditated daily with this little one and traveled the universe with him on a daily basis prior to his death.

My second pregnancy was different as it took every ounce of energy I had to maintain the pregnancy. I could not consciously meditate as the baby's energy would not allow it and I went into pre-term labor at twenty-five weeks gestation. With the help of my spiritual friends and my spiritual guides, we facilitated my son staying inside my physical vessel until I was thirty-eight weeks pregnant.

I must say, I had great concerns that maybe I was not bonding with my son Kyle when I was pregnant with him. My relationship with him was so different when I compared it to my first pregnancy. I knew I had no fear of miscarrying, as the outcome of each pregnancy is not in our hands.

I trusted that God knew what he was doing when he was giving me a second chance. I felt I was doing exactly what I should be doing and not judge the experience. All my energy was completely focused on allowing the pregnancy to happen.

It was only in the last month of my second pregnancy that I was given the information that my son Kyle was in fact the same spirit as the baby I had miscarried. He was an advanced spirit spending a great deal of time on the astral plane along side Archangel Gabriel, and at the same time, he was attached to his little body growing within my uterus.

These insights were comforting, as I fully understood what was happening. My son Kyle was more out of his body than in his body therefore it was difficult to feel his presence. There was no need to bond further with him as the bonding process occurred during the first pregnancy when he was called PP Penny. My main focus within my second pregnancy was trying to maintain a high vibrational frequency to facilitate his physical manifestation.

I felt from the moment my son Kyle was born that he immediately bonded with my husband and it is only now that I can see the reason why. My son Kyle was aware that I would be having a second son so it was in his highest and best interest to bond more with my husband.

He was fully aware that I would be energetically unavailable to him as I embarked on another pregnancy. It was not until after the birth of my second son Bryan that Kyle and I fully bonded.

My second son Bryan's energy is similar to my own energetic constitution making the adjustments required during pregnancy easier for me. I experienced a great deal of sacredness and I found it very easy for me to energetically connect with him. During pregnancy I asked my second son over and over what he wanted to be named, but he did not answer.

I believe our name carries a great deal of power. Kyle gave me his name in late pregnancy. My son Bryan gave me no insight into what he wanted to be called. The only name that sounded right was Ryan. Originally I called him Ryan and within twelve hours of his birth I was unable to remember his name. It was as if it his name was erased from my brain. I thought this was strange. It forced me to meditate with him and he telepathically informed me his name was to be Bryan, not Ryan.

CHAPTER 17

▼

A message from a seven-week old baby for humanity

I conclude this book with a message dictated to me by my son Kyle when he was seven-week's old. Basically, his message summarizes this book. I stand in awe at the level of consciousness of newborn babies. My son's message is grammatically unedited, and this is exactly how the message to humanity was given to me.

At seven-week's post partum, I was awakened from a sound sleep at four in the morning. I heard a voice saying, "Ma wake up, take a pen and paper, and write down this message." This was a very strange occurrence and for a moment I thought, perhaps I flipped and was going crazy! I kept hearing the same sentence over and over again.

I could see a band of energy extend from my body out through the hallway and into my son's room. It was clear to me that I was not going to get any sleep until I followed his instructions. The following is what my son Kyle had to say to humanity.

"My name is Kyle Bajor, and I am exactly seven-weeks old today. I am transmitting this information through the consciousness of my mother. She is a spiritual healer with the ability to telepathically communicate with me. It is important to get this message out to the world, that each of us humans no matter what age we are, choose to be here.

The challenge of being human is the greatest challenge we spiritual beings have to go through. If each individual on this Earth plane were to take self-responsibility for making the decision to be here in physical form, the world would be a different place.

We as spiritual beings, are vast and magnificent beings, with the possibility to be in total harmony with all if we let go of being separate from each other. You see, in the world of spirit, the world we came from there was only oneness and total harmony. It is indeed true that in choosing to become human, we temporary disconnected from the frequency of oneness, and separated down into the human experience.

This separation from oneness is only temporary, and necessary for anchoring the spirit with the physical body. The mistake most humans make is forgetting to reconnect to the oneness as we walk through life. Life is definitely a challenge to all humans but we can decide at any given moment what choices we make.

We can in any given situation, choose from many options, which in turn has a rebound effect. In other words we create our reality. We wrote the book before we came here, and continue to write and re-write the pages depending on choices we make. Knowing this, we can definitely improve upon our lives by taking responsibility for everything we manifest here on the physical plane.

If your life is a mess you created it. Not your mother, your father, or a bad relationship. It is you weaving the web of circumstances you choose to get tangled in, which caused the mess you are sitting in.

My advice to you is to return to the consciousness of infancy when life was so simple, letting go of all external pressures that have accumulated within your life. Think of what it is like to be a seven-week old, and all I seem to do in the outside world is eat, sleep, burp, sometimes cry, pee and poop. Well, there is much more that goes on. As humans we are like computer data banks, always recording and storing data within our systems.

Yes, it is true to say that some of us are luckier than others, that some of us have cleaner data input than others, but so what! We are all here to experience what it is to be human. We choose the experience. We preselected our parents and family members from the state of oneness way before conception.

On a higher level, there was an agreement with the spirit and the soul of our parents that they were the ones, who would be honored, to allow for the facilitation of the creation of your physical body. You single handedly picked your parents. You knew all about them before you decided to physically incarnate.

If you can understand and accept this, you can change a lot about yourself. Taking self-responsibility for the date, time, place and circumstances we choose to incarnate into, is in itself a great healing. Let go of all the wrong done to you, as the truth is all events in your life were written in your life book, by you, before you arrived here.

Now having said that, we can rewrite the book. As I said before, just sit and be in the consciousness of a seven-week old baby. Write down all the wonderful things that you would like to create in this lifetime. Get out there and start manifesting your heart's desires.

A seven-week old baby has no limitations to its imagination and has full conscious awareness of the vastness of the universe. Forgiveness and acceptance is the ERASER used to rewrite your book. Just accept where you are in life and that you created it. Forgive all that have done you wrong, and move on. Constantly reconnect with the oneness of what it was like before you became human and in time you will anchor this oneness into your entire being. This is when you will start to live life to the fullest.

This is what is needed to change the world, one person at a time. We change and those around us change. Everything begins and ends with you! We are all in this together. Honor, love, respect and forgive each other, no matter what page they are acting out from their book.

Love and light, Kyle Bajor"

Telephone Healing Practice

Hannah's private telephone healing practice focuses on assessment and treatment of the fragmented parts of a person's mind, body, soul and spirit. Her unique spiritual gift of "soul reweaving" allows her to locate the emotional traumas within a person or group of people and then reweave these patterns facilitating deep emotional healing.

Hannah is a medical intuitive and has the ability to communicate with the cells of the body, the organs, and the bones. She works with people before and after surgery and chemotherapy to expedite recovery time. People of all ages, from all walks of life and various religious backgrounds seek Hannah's work. She helps bring peace of mind to people who are experiencing difficult times in their lives, regardless of the cause.

Because Hannah's soul type is of direct angelic decent she is connected to the Angels in a very unique way. She has the ability to communicate with babies inside and outside the uterus. She works very well with pregnant women and new mothers helping them to make the adjustment to the role of "mother". She makes no claim of spontaneous healings but will say she "has changed the lives of many people in a very positive way."

Making an appointment for an energetic healing session is simple. Just call to schedule a date and time. At the appointed time, you will phone Hannah (international clients will be phoned by Hannah). During the treatment you are asked to be resting in a comfortable position undisturbed by other family members. Instead of a physical assessment, Hannah will perform a physic assessment of your energy field.

During a healing session it is not unusual for Hannah to receive messages directly from your guides and will share this information with you. Messages range from simple advice to explanations of why you are here on this planet, some of your soul contracts, and how you energetically operate in life on a daily basis. The information received is very profound and will definitely change your outlook on life.

Following a session most clients feel very relaxed, empowered and ready to approach life from a new prospective.

Contact information:

Hannah M. Bajor, C.N.M.,M.S.N.,R.N.C.

Tel: Outside the USA 001-203-272-4791

Tel: Within the USA 1-203-272-4791

Web site: www.timetohealllc.com

Email: hbajor@cox.net

Cover illustrated by Ruthie Basham

Ruthie is a very gifted Personalized Healing Mandala artist, creating mandala's for people all over the world. Her artwork comprises sacred images, symbols, and colors that can be used for powerful personal healing, prayer, meditation, and as a reminder of one's own divinity.

Ruthies mission is to "see through the eyes of God and reflect that back to people. May we all see God in ourselves and in each other".

To order your Personalized Healing Mandala visit:

www.ruthiebasham.com

ISBN 1-41204998-9

9 781412 049986